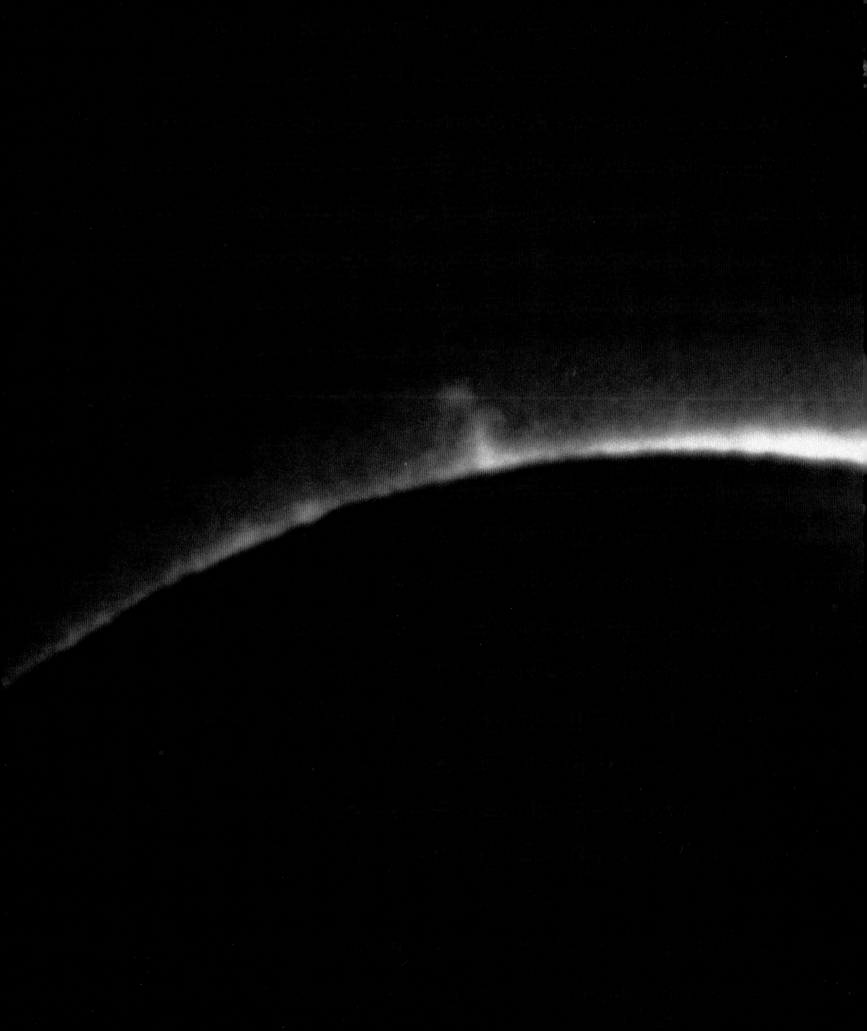

THE SUN

MICHAEL GEORGE

CREATIVE EDUCATION INC.

Designed by Rita Marshall
with the help of Thomas Lawton

© 1991 Creative Education, Inc.
123 South Broad Street,
Mankato, Minnesota 56001

Photography by International
Stock Photography, NASA,
National Optical Astronomy
Observatories, Profiles West,
Rothstein Redstone Associates,
Frank Rossotto, Jerry Sinkovec,
Uniphoto, and Nina Wilmot

Library of Congress
Cataloging-in-Publication Data

George, Michael, 1964–
The Sun / by Michael George.
Summary: Describes the appearance,
activities, and life cycle of the Earth's
source of light and heat.
ISBN 0-88682-402-8
1. Sun—Juvenile literature.
[1. Sun.] I. Title.   90-22255
08521.5.G46   1991   CIP
523.7—dc20   AC

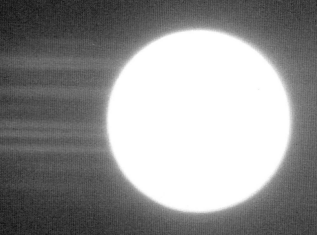

6

Early each morning, the darkness of night slowly fades over the eastern horizon. As the stars disappear, dull blues, shimmering pinks, and brilliant oranges replace the dark, shadowy colors of night. Soon, the glaring yellow *Sun* rises above the horizon and signals the start of a new day.

Sunrise.

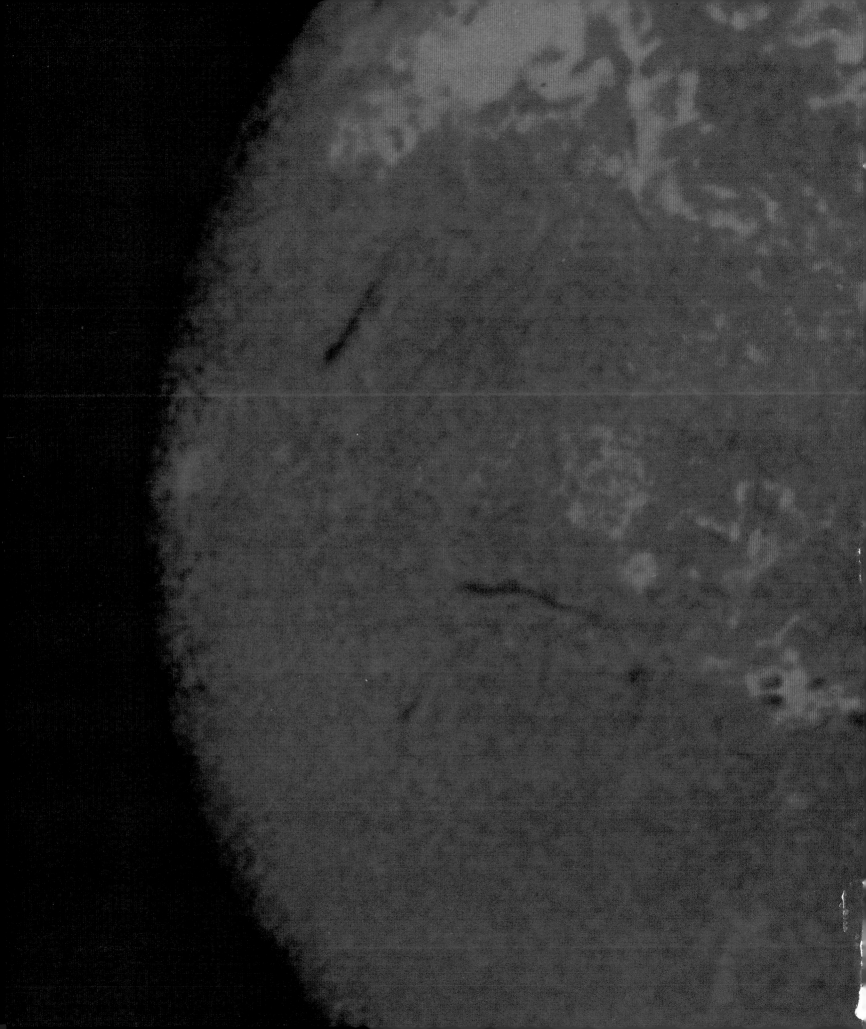

As the day unfolds, the Sun appears to travel across the sky. Not too long ago, people thought the Sun moved across the sky while the Earth stood still. We now know that the Sun's apparent motion is caused by movement of the Earth around the Sun.

❧

The Earth is like a gigantic spinning ball that makes one rotation every twenty-four hours. When we are on the side of the Earth facing the Sun, we have day. As the day progresses, the Earth rotates from west to east and the Sun appears to travel across the sky. Eventually, the Earth's rotation carries us away from the Sun's rays. On Earth, we see the beautiful colors of sunset and watch the sky turn black. Darkness lasts until the next morning, when the Earth's rotation again carries us into the Sun's light.

The Sun.

The brilliant glare of the daytime Sun distinguishes the Sun as a unique object in the sky. Nothing within trillions of miles compares to the Sun in brightness or in size. The Sun is 860,000 miles across—over a hundred times wider than the Earth. If the Sun were hollow, it could hold more than a million Earths.

Yet despite its unique appearance, the Sun is just an ordinary Star. It is no different from the thousands of stars that are visible every night. The Sun appears bigger and brighter than other stars simply because it is the closest star to the Earth. The Sun is 93 million miles from Earth. The next closest star is about 25 trillion miles away, or about three hundred thousand times farther away than the Sun. Other stars are billions of times farther away than this.

Distant stars are like our Sun.

12

Like other stars, the Sun is an enormous ball of hot, glowing gases. The gases are hottest right at the center, or core, of the Sun. Temperatures at the core are about 27 million degrees Fahrenheit. At this temperature, tiny hydrogen atoms in the Sun "melt" together to form atoms of helium. This process, called *Nuclear Fusion,* is similar to a continuous hydrogen bomb explosion. Nuclear fusion releases tremendous amounts of heat and light, causing the Sun to shine.

Nuclear fusion makes sunshine.

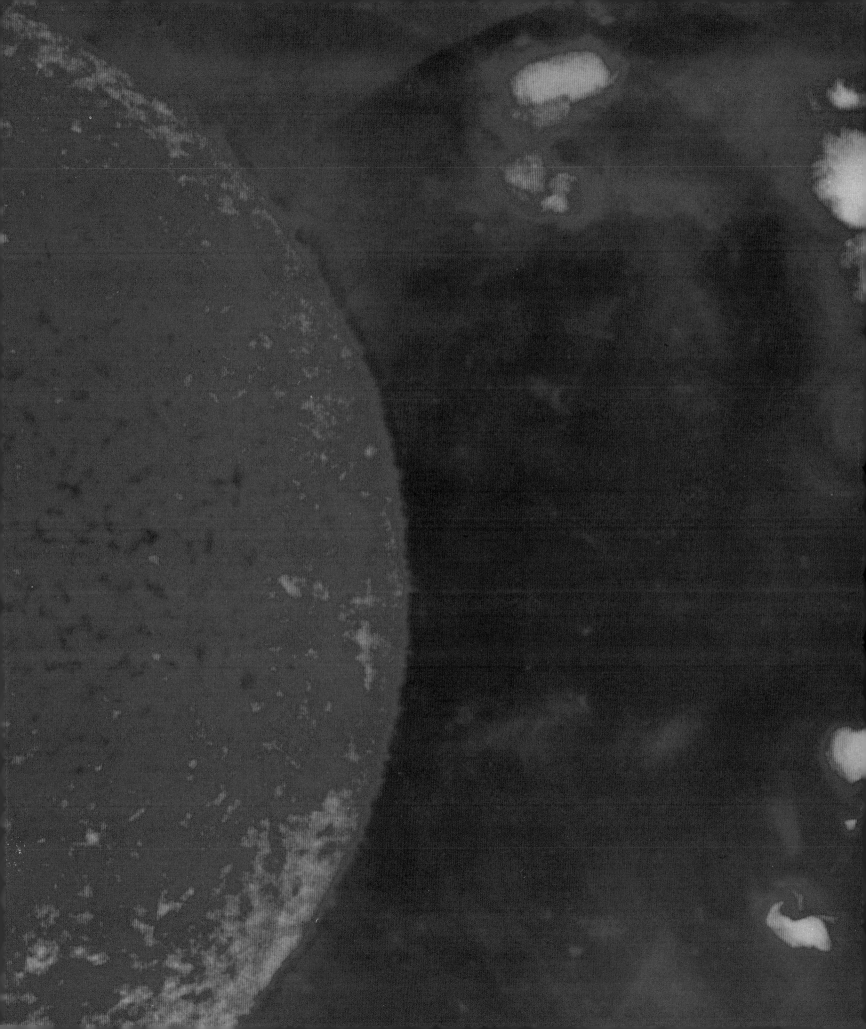

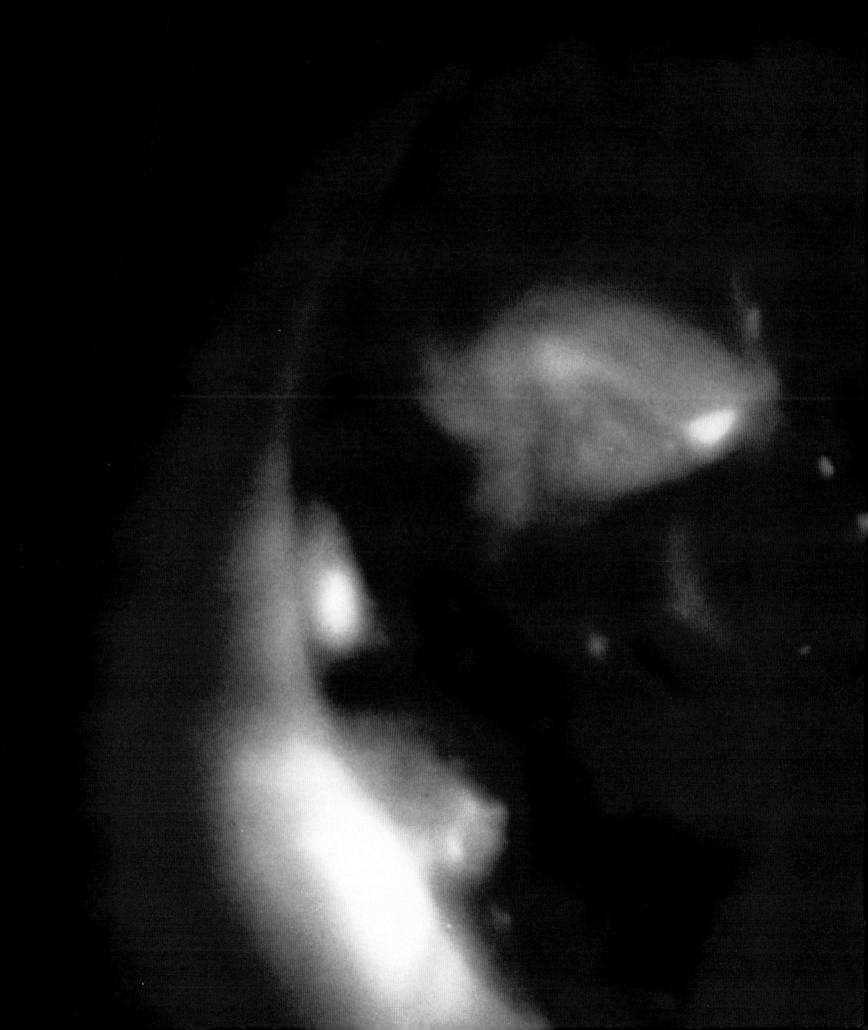

15

The temperature on the Sun's surface is 10,000 degrees Fahrenheit, much cooler than the core, but still extremely hot. The Sun's surface is so hot that any substance—even rock or metal—would melt and boil away into gases if it were brought to the Sun. Therefore, the surface of the Sun is not solid like the surface of the Earth. Instead, it is the point at which the immensely hot gases of the Sun's interior meet the relatively cooler gases of the Sun's atmosphere.

The surface of the Sun.

The surface of the Sun is not as smooth and featureless as it appears from the Earth. Turbulence inside the Sun creates waves of gas, called *Granules,* that dot the entire surface. Although they appear tiny from Earth, a typical granule is one thousand miles in diameter, larger than the state of Texas. Like waves on the ocean, individual granules last only a few moments, but as soon as one disappears, another takes its place.

Solar granules cover the surface.

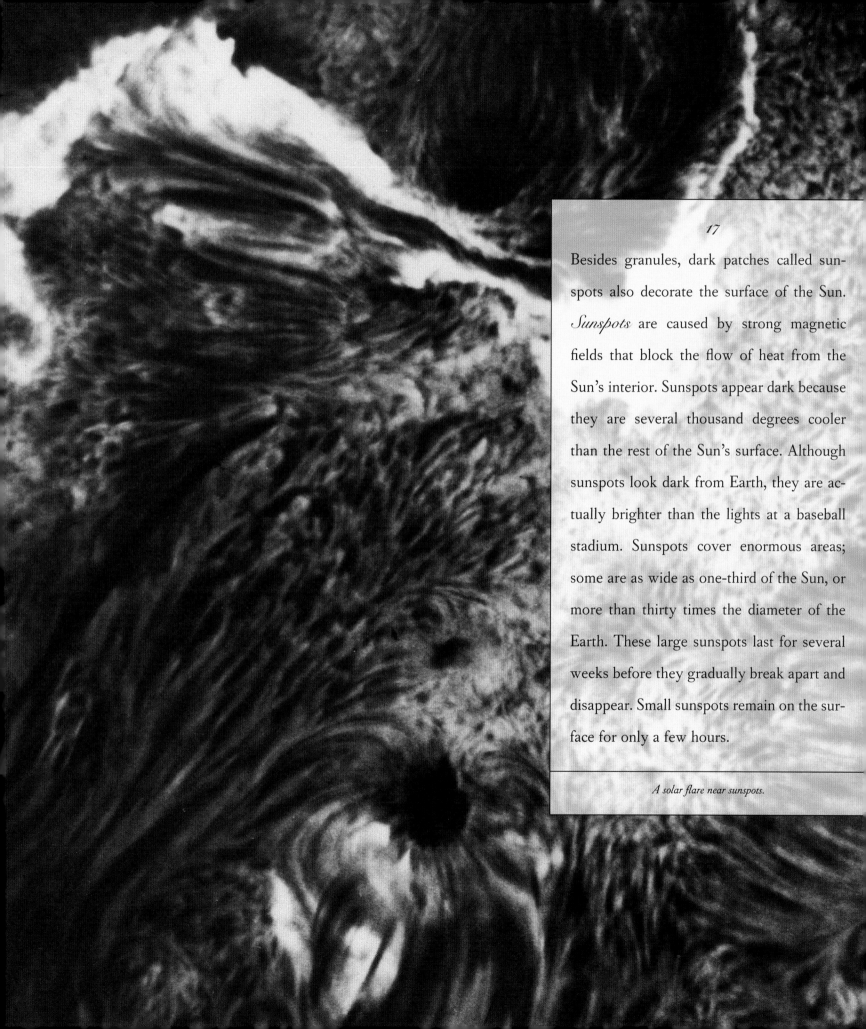

17

Besides granules, dark patches called sunspots also decorate the surface of the Sun. *Sunspots* are caused by strong magnetic fields that block the flow of heat from the Sun's interior. Sunspots appear dark because they are several thousand degrees cooler than the rest of the Sun's surface. Although sunspots look dark from Earth, they are actually brighter than the lights at a baseball stadium. Sunspots cover enormous areas; some are as wide as one-third of the Sun, or more than thirty times the diameter of the Earth. These large sunspots last for several weeks before they gradually break apart and disappear. Small sunspots remain on the surface for only a few hours.

A solar flare near sunspots.

19

Occasionally, spectacular eruptions called *solar flares* burst forth from sunspots. A Solar Flare sends waves of intense heat, light, and radiation far into space. The energy from a solar flare reaches the Earth in about two days. When the radiation enters the Earth's atmosphere, it makes electric lights flicker and may disrupt radio communications and telephone calls.

Page 18: A sunspot.
Page 19: A solar flare.

Flares also thrust tiny particles into space. The particles ejected from a solar flare collide with gases far above the poles of the Earth. The collisions release energy and cause the air to glow, producing the beautiful *Polar Lights*. The polar lights are visible at night near the poles of the Earth. They appear as shimmering arches, curtains, or rays that seem to dance against the dark night sky. Although the polar lights are usually white or greenish-yellow, they can pulsate with all the colors of the rainbow.

Polar lights seen from space.

In addition to granules, sunspots, and solar flares, huge sheets of glowing gas, called *Prominences,* also originate on the surface of the Sun. Unlike solar flares, which erupt forcefully, solar prominences hang loosely above the surface of the Sun. While a typical prominence extends for twenty thousand miles above the Sun's surface, some reach altitudes of over three hundred thousand miles.

Solar Prominences.

Like the Earth, the Sun is surrounded by a thin cloud of gases called an atmosphere. The largest prominences barely reach the outermost layer of the Sun's atmosphere, the *Solar Corona*. The solar corona spreads out into space for millions of miles. In fact, the Earth itself is surrounded by the Sun's corona. Although it is enormous, the solar corona is visible only during a total solar eclipse, when the Moon crosses directly between the Sun and the Earth. Only then is the brilliant glare of the Sun blocked and the fainter glow of the corona revealed. On average, total solar eclipses occur somewhere on Earth only once every year and a half.

Page 24: A moment after total eclipse.
Pages 24-25: The solar corona during a total eclipse.

The Sun supplies us with all the energy we need for the basic functions of life. It also supplies us with the energy we need to power our societies. Coal generates electricity, oil powers our cars, and natural gas heats our homes. These forms of energy, called *Fossil Fuels,* are derived from the remains of plants and animals that lived millions of years ago. These organisms could not have lived without energy from the Sun. Whenever we turn on a light, start a car, or heat a building, we release the Sun's energy, stored for millions of years in the remains of ancient organisms.

The Sun is our most basic energy source.

34

The Sun has warmed our world and lighted our skies for billions of years. However, as reliable as the Sun seems, it cannot shine forever. Five billion years from now the Sun will slowly run out of hydrogen fuel. As it does, the Sun will begin to contract, squeezing the core tighter and tighter. As pressure inside the Sun grows, temperatures in the core will rise higher than ever before. Eventually, the interior of the Sun will become so hot that the Sun will burst like a piece of popcorn, growing hundreds of times larger than it is today.

The Sun's core will become hotter.

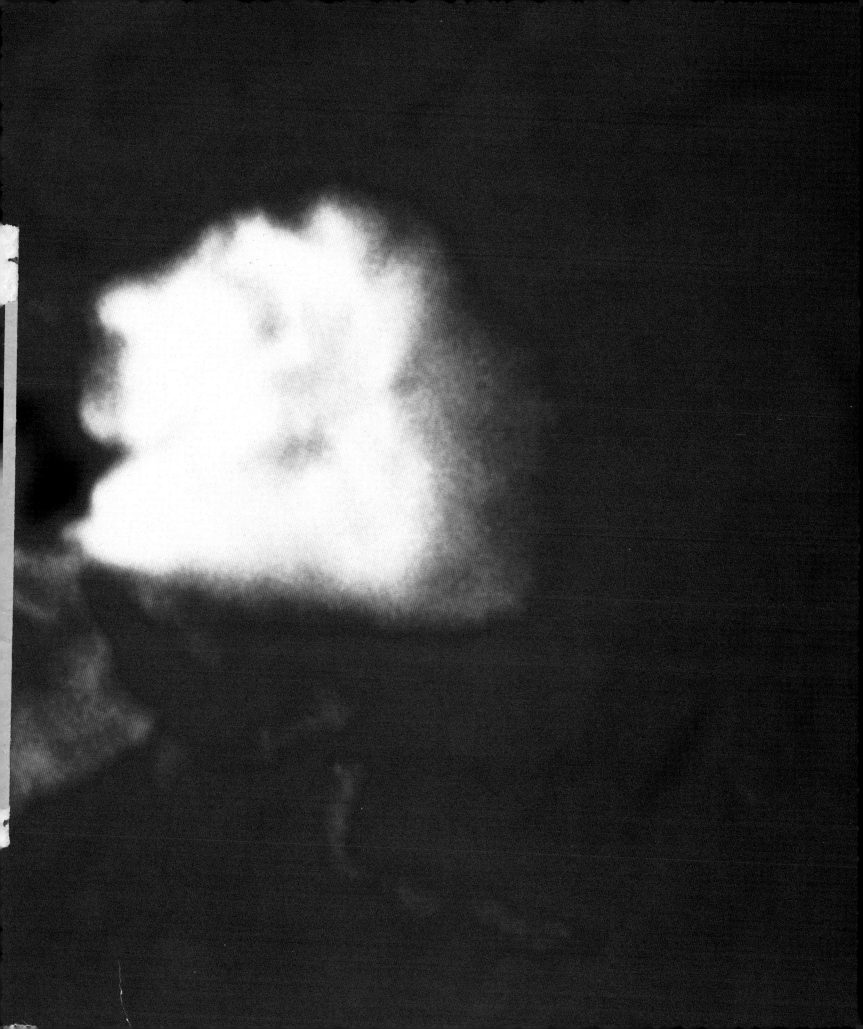

36

As the Sun swells in size, temperatures on Earth will soar. The unbearable temperatures will melt the Earth's polar ice caps, and water will flood the continents. The Sun, still growing, will fill half of the daytime sky. Before long, the Earth's oceans will begin to boil and eventually evaporate. No longer covered with water, the surface of the Earth will melt into molten lava. Life will cease to exist on the face of the Earth.

The Earth's surface.

39

Eventually, the Sun's outer layers will be thrust into space. The thick cloud of gases will drift away from the Sun's remaining core, which will have shrunk to the size of the Earth. By then, all of the Sun's fuel will be used up, but the Sun will continue to glow simply because it is hot. Over thousands of years, the Sun will lose its heat into space and will finally turn cold and dark.

Nebulae are the result of an exploded star.

40

Until *The Sun* becomes a cold, dark globe floating through space, creatures on Earth will continue to bask in its heat and humankind will continue to contemplate its existence. For now, the surface of the Sun is constantly erupting with activity. Sunspots dot the surface, solar prominences hang high in the atmosphere, and solar flares shoot far into space. In its beauty and brilliance, the Sun holds much intrigue; in its heat and light, the Sun radiates the energy of life.

A solar eruption.